Lerner *SPORTS*

G.O.A.T.

HOCKEY TEAMS

Copyright © 2021 by Lerner Publishing Group, Inc.

All rights reserved. International copyright secured. No part of this book may be reproduced, stored in a retrieval system, or transmitted in any form or by any means—electronic, mechanical, photocopying, recording, or otherwise—without the prior written permission of Lerner Publishing Group, Inc., except for the inclusion of brief quotations in an acknowledged review.

Lerner Publications Company
An imprint of Lerner Publishing Group, Inc.
241 First Avenue North
Minneapolis, MN 55401 USA

For reading levels and more information, look up this title at www.lernerbooks.com.

Main body text set in Aptifer Sans LT Pro.Typeface provided by Linotype AG.

Designer: Kimberly Morales

Library of Congress Cataloging-in-Publication Data

Names: Doeden, Matt, author.
Title: G.O.A.T. hockey teams / Matt Doeden.
Description: Minneapolis : Lerner Publications, 2021 | Series: Greatest of all time teams (Lerner sports) | Includes bibliographical references and index. | Audience: Ages 7–11 | Audience: Grades 2–3 | Summary: "In 2019, the Tampa Bay Lightning tied the 1976–1977 Montreal Canadiens for most wins in a season. Which teams are the greatest of all time? Compare their stats and greatest moments and decide for yourself"—Provided by publisher.
Identifiers: LCCN 2020010380 (print) | LCCN 2020010381 (ebook) | ISBN 9781728404448 (library binding) | ISBN 9781728418247 (ebook)
Subjects: LCSH: Hockey—Records—Juvenile literature. | Hockey teams—Juvenile literature. | Hockey players—Juvenile literature.
Classification: LCC GV847.25 .D645 2021 (print) | LCC GV847.25 (ebook) | DDC 796.962—dc23

LC record available at https://lccn.loc.gov/2020010380
LC ebook record available at https://lccn.loc.gov/2020010381

Manufactured in the United States of America
1-48502-49016-9/9/2020

TABLE OF CONTENTS

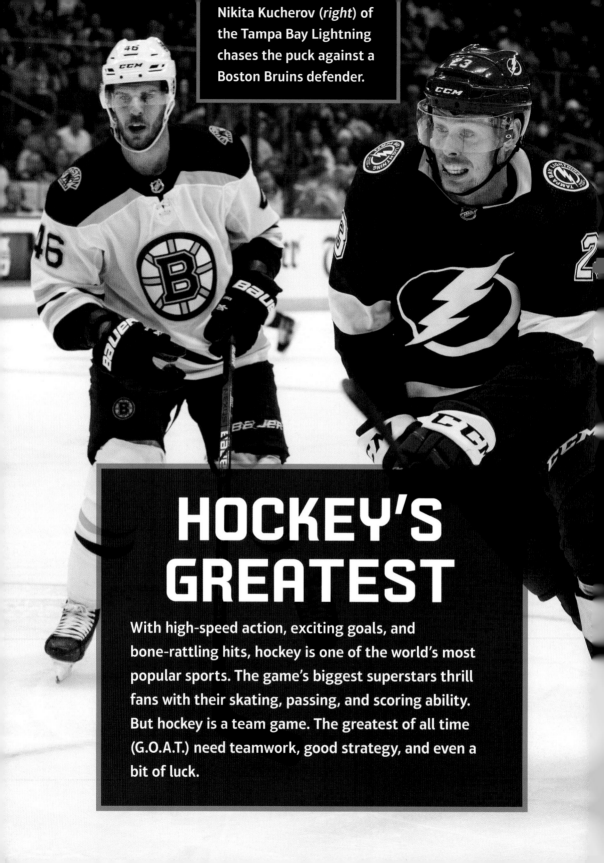

Nikita Kucherov (*right*) of the Tampa Bay Lightning chases the puck against a Boston Bruins defender.

HOCKEY'S GREATEST

With high-speed action, exciting goals, and bone-rattling hits, hockey is one of the world's most popular sports. The game's biggest superstars thrill fans with their skating, passing, and scoring ability. But hockey is a team game. The greatest of all time (G.O.A.T.) need teamwork, good strategy, and even a bit of luck.

FACTS AT A GLANCE

>> The Tampa Bay Lightning tied a National Hockey League (NHL) record with 62 regular-season wins in 2018–2019. But they failed to win a single playoff game.

>> From 2002 to 2014, the Canada National Women's Team won four straight Olympic gold medals.

>> Six members of the 1984–1985 Edmonton Oilers scored at least 20 goals.

>> In the early 1980s, the New York Islanders won four straight Stanley Cup titles.

>> The 1955–1956 Montreal Canadiens roster included 11 future members of the Hockey Hall of Fame.

The NHL is the highest level of pro hockey in the world. Players from all around the globe compete to win hockey's biggest prize, the Stanley Cup. Teams earn their place in the playoffs during a long regular season. Then they must survive three rounds of playoff games to reach the Stanley Cup Finals.

Many top players also play on national teams. Some countries build a team of all-stars to compete at international events such as the Olympic Games. The action is intense. Fans go wild with every goal. Only one nation can win it all and stake a claim as the best in the world.

Boston's Charlie McAvoy (*right*) and Tyler Bozak of the St. Louis Blues battle for control of the puck.

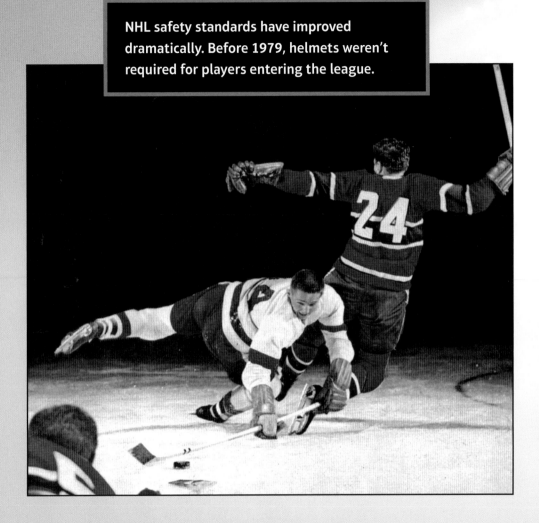

NHL safety standards have improved dramatically. Before 1979, helmets weren't required for players entering the league.

But what makes a team great? Is it record-setting performances and regular-season success? Or do championships define greatness?

Hockey has changed a lot over the decades. How do fans compare a team from the 1950s to one from the 2020s? How do they compare a national team to an NHL squad? As you learn more about the G.O.A.T. teams, think about how you'd compare them. Then decide the G.O.A.T. for yourself.

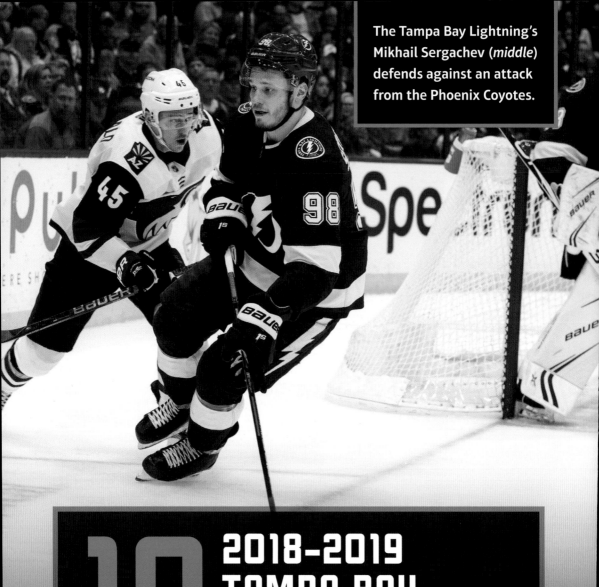

The Tampa Bay Lightning's Mikhail Sergachev (*middle*) defends against an attack from the Phoenix Coyotes.

NO. 10
2018–2019 TAMPA BAY LIGHTNING

The 2018–2019 Tampa Bay Lightning were unstoppable. With the league's top offense and fifth-ranked defense, they had it all. Nikita Kucherov, Steven Stamkos, and Brayden Point scored almost at will.

Tampa Bay blazed through the regular season. They won 62 games, tied for the most in NHL history. The Lightning looked like they could stake a claim as the greatest team of all time.

Then came the playoffs, where everything went horribly wrong. The Lightning faced the Columbus Blue Jackets. Columbus had struggled even to make the playoffs. But Tampa Bay's powerful offense dried up against the Blue Jackets. Columbus swept the Lightning in four games. After tying the record for wins in the regular season, the Lightning failed to win a single playoff game. It was one of the biggest upsets in sports history. But despite their playoff flop, the Lightning's amazing regular season makes them one of the greatest of all time.

Nikita Kucherov

2018-2019 LIGHTNING STATS

- ➤➤➤ Tampa Bay went 32–7–2 at home.
- ➤➤➤ They won 10 games in a row from February 9 to February 27.
- ➤➤➤ The Lightning outscored their opponents 325–222 in the regular season.
- ➤➤➤ Nikita Kucherov led the team with 128 points.
- ➤➤➤ Tampa Bay's 62 regular-season wins were 12 more than the next best team.

Athletes bring their all to the ice at the 2018 Winter Olympic Games.

NO. 9 2018 US WOMEN'S NATIONAL TEAM

Canada was the major force in women's hockey during the 2000s. Team Canada had won four straight gold medals entering the 2018 Winter Olympics. But a new power was ready to take them down: Team USA.

Canada beat the US Women's National Team in the group round. But that was the only game the US lost. Both teams advanced to the knockout round. They were on a collision course for the title.

The gold-medal game was one for the ages. The two powerful teams traded shot after shot. After three periods, they were locked in a 2–2 tie. Nobody scored in a 20-minute overtime period. That sent the game to a shoot-out.

The teams remained tied after five rounds. Fans roared as skaters came out for the sixth round. Jocelyne Lamoureux-Davidson blasted a goal for Team USA. Then US goalie Maddie Rooney stopped Canada's final shot, giving the United States the victory.

Maddie Rooney

2018 TEAM USA STATS

▸▸▸ The US Women's National Team outscored their opponents 17–5 in the Olympics.

▸▸▸ Jocelyne Lamoureux-Davidson and Dani Cameranesi led the team with five points each.

▸▸▸ Maddie Rooney led Olympic goalies by averaging 1.16 goals allowed per game.

▸▸▸ Team USA's victory snapped Canada's streak of four straight gold medals.

▸▸▸ It was Team USA's first Olympic gold medal since 1998.

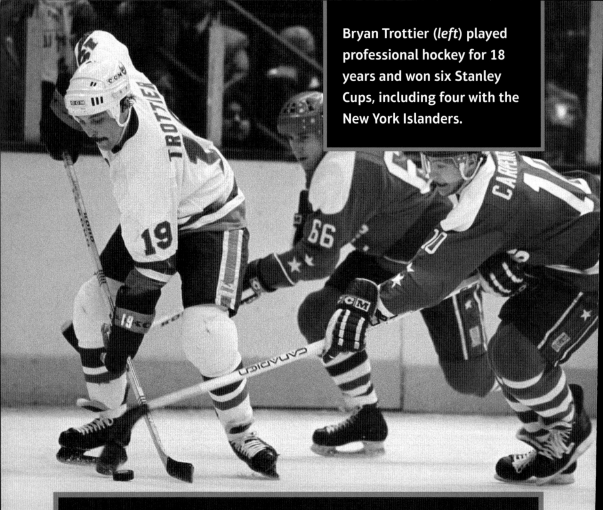

Bryan Trottier (*left*) played professional hockey for 18 years and won six Stanley Cups, including four with the New York Islanders.

NO. 8

1982-1983 NEW YORK ISLANDERS

In the early 1980s, no team could match the New York Islanders. From 1980 to 1983, they won four straight Stanley Cup titles. The 1982–1983 team was the peak of their dynasty.

Mike Bossy led a powerful scoring attack. He scored 60 times in the regular season and helped the Islanders average almost four goals per game. But the team's real

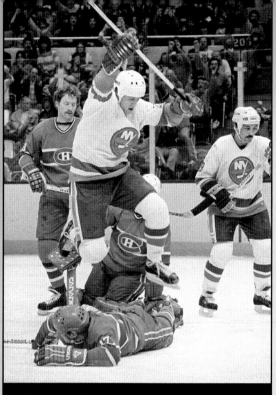

Mike Bossy leaps over an opponent on the ice.

strength was their physical shutdown defense. They allowed just 226 goals, the fewest in the league.

After a 42–26–12 regular season, the Islanders dominated in the playoffs. In 20 playoff games, they outscored their opponents 94–53. They swept the powerful Edmonton Oilers in the Stanley Cup Finals to claim their fourth straight championship. The victory secured their place among the greatest teams in NHL history.

1982-1983 ISLANDERS STATS

>>> Mike Bossy led the team with 60 goals and 118 points.

>>> Goalie Billy Smith won 13 games in the playoffs and was named the playoffs' most valuable player.

>>> The Islanders went 26–11–3 on their home ice during the regular season.

>>> After losing the first game of the season, they won the next eight games in a row.

>>> They outscored the Oilers 17–6 to sweep the Stanley Cup Finals.

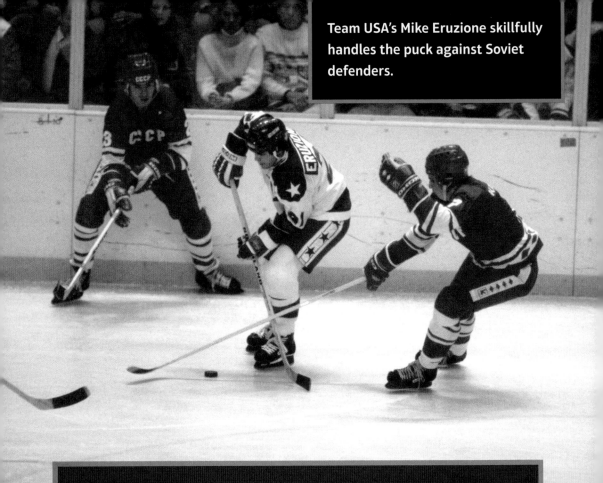

Team USA's Mike Eruzione skillfully handles the puck against Soviet defenders.

1980 US MEN'S NATIONAL TEAM

The United States men's team wasn't the top-ranked team at the 1980 Winter Olympics. It was a group of young, untested players. Few fans expected Team USA to compete for the gold medal. The Soviet Union, a former country that included Russia, had by far the best team at the Olympics. It was made up of pro players who were older and more experienced than their opponents. The Soviets were wiping out every team in their path.

Mark Johnson helped Team USA pull off the Miracle on Ice.

But one game changed everything. Team USA faced the Soviet Union in the semifinal round. The Soviets had outscored their opponents 51–11 in five Olympic victories. Yet the Americans trailed by just one goal late in the game.

Team USA's Mark Johnson tied it with a goal. Then Mike Eruzione shocked everyone by giving Team USA the lead. The young, excited Americans held off the Soviet attack to win the game. The Miracle on Ice remains one of the biggest upsets in sports history. Two days later, the US beat Finland to win the gold medal.

1980 TEAM USA STATS

>>> The average age of Team USA's players was 22.

>>> The United States outscored their opponents 33–15 in the Olympics.

>>> Mark Johnson led the team with 11 points.

>>> Twelve of the team's 20 players were from Minnesota.

>>> Thirteen players later joined the NHL. Mike Eruzione never played another official hockey game.

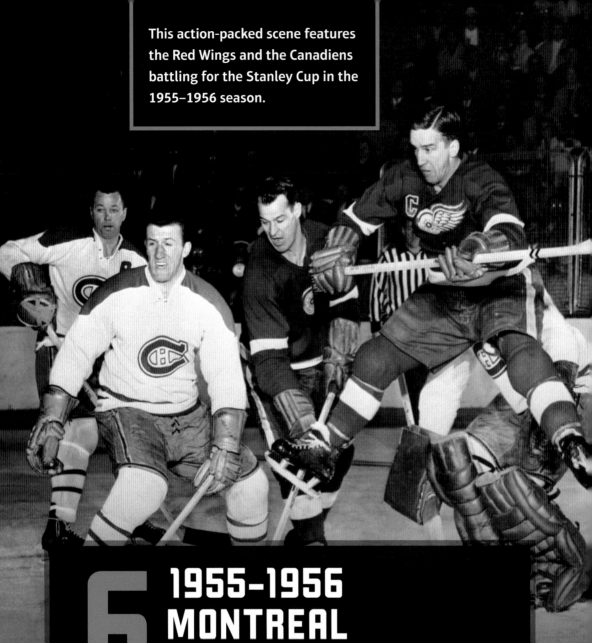

This action-packed scene features the Red Wings and the Canadiens battling for the Stanley Cup in the 1955–1956 season.

NO. 6

1955-1956 MONTREAL CANADIENS

The Montreal Canadiens of the late 1950s were one of hockey's first great dynasties. And they were never better than in 1955–1956. The Canadiens played well at both ends of the rink, leading the NHL in offense and defense. Montreal rolled through the NHL regular season to a 45–15–10 record.

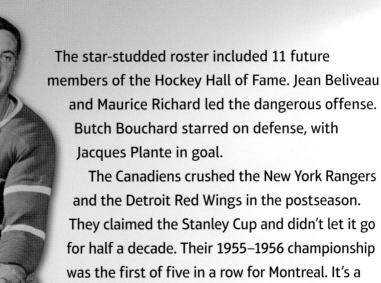

The star-studded roster included 11 future members of the Hockey Hall of Fame. Jean Beliveau and Maurice Richard led the dangerous offense. Butch Bouchard starred on defense, with Jacques Plante in goal.

The Canadiens crushed the New York Rangers and the Detroit Red Wings in the postseason. They claimed the Stanley Cup and didn't let it go for half a decade. Their 1955–1956 championship was the first of five in a row for Montreal. It's a streak that no other NHL team has ever matched.

Jean Beliveau

1955-1956 CANADIENS STATS

>>> Montreal outscored their opponents 222–131 in the regular season.

>>> They won 15 more games than second-place Detroit.

>>> Jean Beliveau led the team in goals (47) and points (88).

>>> The Canadiens went 8–2 in the postseason.

>>> It was Montreal's seventh Stanley Cup championship.

Grant Fuhr was a star goaltender for the Oilers.

5

_{NO.}

1984-1985 EDMONTON OILERS

The Edmonton Oilers were hockey's best team in the 1980s. Hockey legends Wayne Gretzky, Paul Coffey, and Jari Kurri led a furious scoring attack. Goalie Grant Fuhr shut down opposing offenses.

The 1984–1985 season was Edmonton's finest. Gretzky dazzled with a league-leading 208 points. The Oilers went 49–20–11 for the second-best record in the NHL.

Edmonton really turned it on in the playoffs. They went 15–3 in the postseason, controlling almost every game they played. That included a nine-game winning streak to open the playoffs.

The Oilers faced the Philadelphia Flyers in the Stanley Cup Finals. Philly stunned the Oilers by winning Game 1. But Edmonton won the next four games to claim the Stanley Cup. In 2017, fans voted the 1984–1985 Oilers to be the greatest NHL team of all time.

Wayne Gretzky

1984–1985 OILERS STATS

>>> Wayne Gretzky had 135 assists, breaking his own NHL record.

>>> The Oilers outscored other teams 401–298 in the regular season.

>>> Six Oilers players scored 20 or more goals. Grezky led the way with 73.

>>> Edmonton went 26–7–7 at home in the regular season.

>>> Jari Kurri set a record by scoring 12 goals in a postseason series against the Chicago Blackhawks.

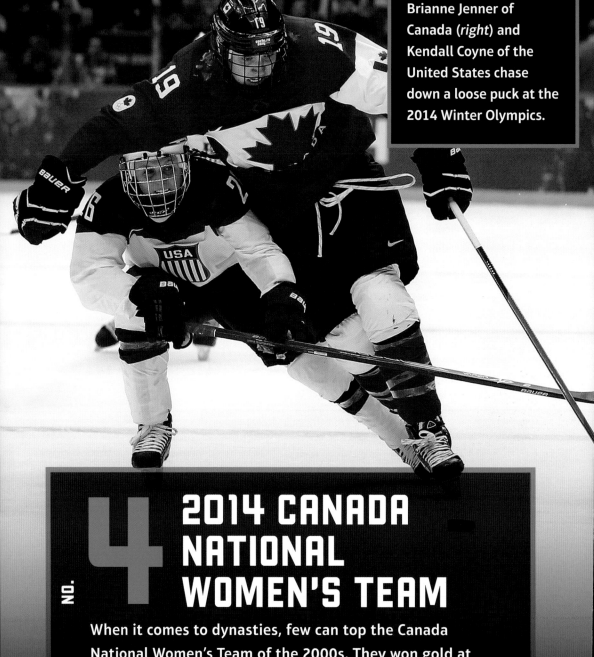

Brianne Jenner of Canada (*right*) and Kendall Coyne of the United States chase down a loose puck at the 2014 Winter Olympics.

NO. 4 2014 CANADA NATIONAL WOMEN'S TEAM

When it comes to dynasties, few can top the Canada National Women's Team of the 2000s. They won gold at the Winter Olympics in 2002, 2006, and 2010. In 2014, the team set out to make it four gold medals in a row. Team Canada had tough defense and great goaltending from Shannon Szabados. They rolled through group play. Canada outscored their opponents 11–2 in three games.

Goaltender Shannon Szabados deftly blocks a shot at the 2014 Winter Olympic Games.

Canada beat Switzerland 3–1 in the knockout round. That set up an epic game with Team USA. It was a gold-medal classic. Canada trailed by two goals late in the game. But they stormed back to force overtime. Then Canada's Marie-Philip Poulin buried the game-winner to complete the amazing comeback. It was the most exciting gold-medal game in women's hockey history. The win helped Canada stake its claim as one of the greatest teams of all time.

2014 TEAM CANADA STATS

- ▶▶▶ Canada won their fourth straight gold medal.
- ▶▶▶ They outscored their opponents 17–5 in five Olympic Games.
- ▶▶▶ In the gold medal game, they scored two goals in the final four minutes to send it to overtime.
- ▶▶▶ Shannon Szabados averaged less than one goal allowed per game.
- ▶▶▶ The United States was the only team to hold a lead against Canada at the Olympics.

The Red Wings were a force to be reckoned with in 2001–2002.

NO. 3 2001-2002 DETROIT RED WINGS

The 2001–2002 Detroit Red Wings roster had some of the greatest players in hockey. The team's nine future Hall of Famers included Sergei Fedorov, Brett Hull, Nicklas Lidstrom, Brendan Shanahan, and Dominik Hasek. It's no wonder they put together one of the most amazing seasons in NHL history.

The Red Wings cruised through the regular season with a quick-strike offense and a tough defense. They won eight of their first nine games. Then they just kept winning. Detroit had by far the best record in the league when they rolled into the playoffs.

The Red Wings fell behind in the first round. They lost their first two games to the Vancouver Canucks. But Detroit stormed back to win the series. They advanced to the Finals and crushed the Carolina Hurricanes four games to one. The title sealed their place among hockey's all-time greats.

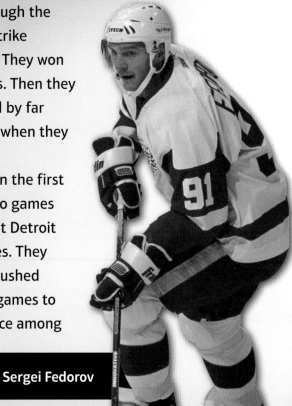

Sergei Fedorov

2001-2002 RED WINGS STATS

>>> Detroit won 51 games, the most in the 2001-2002 regular season.

>>> They outscored other teams 251–187 during the regular season.

>>> The team's head coach, Scotty Bowman, won nine Stanley Cup championships.

>>> Brendan Shanahan led the team with 37 goals.

>>> The Red Wings went 41–15–8 in games started by goalie Dominik Hasek.

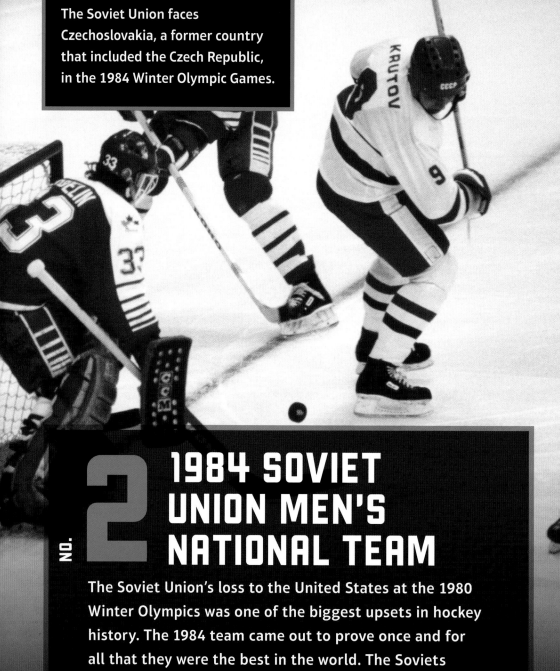

The Soviet Union faces Czechoslovakia, a former country that included the Czech Republic, in the 1984 Winter Olympic Games.

NO.

NO. 2 1984 SOVIET UNION MEN'S NATIONAL TEAM

The Soviet Union's loss to the United States at the 1980 Winter Olympics was one of the biggest upsets in hockey history. The 1984 team came out to prove once and for all that they were the best in the world. The Soviets were loaded. Aleksandr Kozhevnikov, Slava Fetisov, and Vladimir Krutov were scoring machines. Vladislav Tretiak was one of the greatest goalies in the world.

Vladislav Tretiak stopped puck after puck for the Soviet Union.

The Soviets destroyed almost every team they played. They opened the Olympics with a 12–1 blowout of Poland to set the tone. The only close game they played was the gold medal match. They beat Czechoslovakia, 2–0. The Soviet Union claimed gold and got revenge for their shocking loss four years earlier. No team before or since has come close to matching them in Olympic hockey.

1984 TEAM SOVIET UNION STATS

>>> The Soviet Union scored 48 goals and allowed just five in the Olympics.

>>> No team scored more than one goal against them.

>>> Goalie Vladislav Tretiak stopped 112 of the 116 shots he faced.

>>> Slava Fetisov led the team with 11 points.

>>> It was their fifth gold medal in six Winter Olympics.

The Montreal Canadiens dominated in 1976–1977.

1976–1977 MONTREAL CANADIENS

The 1976–1977 Montreal Canadiens were the greatest force in hockey history. They had it all, including nine future Hall of Famers. Guy Lafleur and Steve Shutt were an unstoppable scoring pair. Goalie Ken Dryden blocked almost every shot that came his way. The Canadiens opened the season with a 10–1 victory over the Pittsburgh Penguins and never looked back. They went on to set 21 NHL records.

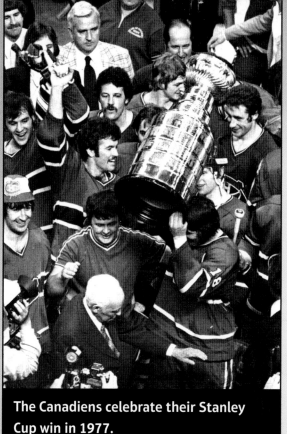

The Canadiens celebrate their Stanley Cup win in 1977.

In the regular season, the Canadiens won 11 more games than any other team. They were even better in the playoffs. Montreal went 12–2 on their way to winning the Stanley Cup. That included a four-game sweep of the Boston Bruins in the Finals. The Canadiens lifted the Stanley Cup to celebrate the greatest season in hockey history.

1976–1977 CANADIENS STATS

>>> The Canadiens went 60–8–12 in the regular season.

>>> They outscored other teams 387–171 in the regular season.

>>> Guy Lafleur led the team with 136 points.

>>> Goalie Ken Dryden had a 41–6–8 record. Backup goalie Michel Larocque's record was 19–2–4.

>>> The Canadiens outscored the Bruins 16–6 in the Finals.

YOUR
G.O.A.T.

ASK 10 FANS TO MAKE THEIR OWN LIST OF HOCKEY'S GREATEST TEAMS AND YOU'LL PROBABLY GET 10 DIFFERENT LISTS. That's because there's no right or wrong way to rank teams from different eras and leagues. As you learn more about some of hockey's greatest teams, you may form your own opinions about them.

What do you value most? Is it playoff wins and Stanley Cup championships? Or do great regular seasons carry more weight? Do you look for teams with rosters loaded with Hall-of-Fame talent? What about record-setting performances?

If you disagree with this list, make your own! Check out books and websites on hockey's greatest teams and players. Talk to fellow hockey fans about who they consider the greatest. Come up with your own top 10, and crown your own greatest of all time. Then have a friend do the same and compare your results. Where do you agree? Where do you disagree?

HOCKEY FACTS

>>> The Stanley Cup existed long before the NHL. Early on, any team could challenge for the cup, even teams from other leagues.

>>> Manon Rhéaume is the only woman to play for an NHL team. She played goalie for the Tampa Bay Lightning in preseason games in the early 1990s.

>>> In 1920, Joe Malone of the Quebec Bulldogs scored seven goals in an NHL game, setting a record that still stands.

>>> No one has scored more career goals than Wayne Gretzky's 894. He also holds the all-time record for assists with 1,963.

GLOSSARY

assist: a pass that leads to a goal

dynasty: a long period of dominance by a team, usually including multiple championships

group round: the stage of a tournament in which teams in a group play one another. The top teams advance to the knockout round.

knockout round: the stage of a tournament in which the winning team advances and the losing team is knocked out of the tournament

point: a goal or assist

postseason: a period of time immediately after the regular season when teams play to determine a champion

regular season: the main part of a sports season during which all teams play

roster: a list of players on a team

shoot-out: a system that uses penalty shots to determine the winner of a game that is tied after overtime

upset: an unexpected victory

LEARN MORE

Fishman, Jon M. *Hockey's G.O.A.T.: Wayne Gretzky, Sidney Crosby, and More*. Minneapolis: Lerner Publications, 2020.

Ice Hockey—Winter Olympic Sport
https://www.olympic.org/ice-hockey

Monson, James. *Behind the Scenes Hockey*. Minneapolis: Lerner Publications, 2020.

National Hockey League
https://www.nhl.com/

Sports Illustrated Kids—Hockey
https://www.sikids.com/hockey

Walker, Jason M. *Crosby vs. Ovechkin vs. McDavid vs. Gretzky*. New York: Rosen Central, 2020.

INDEX

PHOTO ACKNOWLEDGMENTS

Image credits: Dave Sandford/Allsport/Getty Images, p. 1; Scott Audette/NHLI/Getty Images, pp. 4, 8; AP Photo/Charles Krupa, p. 6; Bruce Bennett Studios/Getty Images, pp. 7, 15, 18, 19; Patrick Smith/Getty Images, p. 9; BRENDAN SMIALOWSKI/AFP/Getty Images, p. 10; Harry How/Getty Images, pp. 11, 21; AP Photo/Richard Drew, p. 12; AP Photo/G. Paul Burnett, p. 13; Focus on Sport/Getty Images, p. 14; Bettmann/Getty Images, pp. 16, 17; AP Photo/Matt Slocum, p. 20; Elsa/NHLI/Getty Images, p. 22; Jeff Vinnick/Allsport/Getty Images, p. 23; Wally McNamee/Corbis Historical/Getty Images, p. 24; Eileen Langsley/Popperfoto/Getty Images, p. 25; Denis Brodeur/NHLI/Getty Images, p. 26; Frank O'Brien/The Boston Globe/Getty Images, p. 27; aperturesound/Shutterstock.com, p. 28 (puck). Design elements: ijaydesign99/Shutterstock.com; RaiDztor/Shutterstock.com; MIKHAIL GRACHIKOV/Shutterstock.com; EFKS/Shutterstock.com; Vitalii Kozyrskyi/Shutterstock.com; ESB Professional/Shutterstock.com; MEandMO/Shutterstock.com; Roman Sotola/Shutterstock.com.

Cover: Dave Sandford/Allsport/Getty Images. Design elements: EFKS/Shutterstock.com; RaiDztor/Shutterstock.com; MIKHAIL GRACHIKOV/Shutterstock.com; ijaydesign99/Shutterstock.com.